BOLD KIDS

Pennsylvania

CHILDREN'S AMERICAN LOCAL HISTORY BOOK

No part of this book may be reproduced or used in any way or form or by any means whether electronic or mechanical, this means that you cannot record or photocopy any material ideas or tips that are provided in this book.
Copyright 2022

All images in this book have been reproduced with the knowledge and prior consent of the artists concerned, and no responsibility is accepted by producer, publisher, or printer for any infringement of copyright or otherwise, arising from the contents of this publication.

Learn more about the state of Pennsylvania with our collection of Facts about the State for kids. This historical state is also known as the Quaker State. The motto of the state is Virtue, Liberty, and Independence.

The official state flower is the mountain laurel, and its state bird is the ruffed goose. The list goes on! Read on for some interesting facts about Pennsylvania!

There are many interesting facts about Pennsylvania. The state's apple-growing region alone is home to 21,000 acres. The state also grows apples, which are grown in every county. While there are no official state vegetables, you can visit the Philadelphia Zoo to see animals.

This was the first public zoo in the country and was founded by Benjamin Franklin. The Independence Bell is the only one of the original thirteen colonies without the Atlantic Ocean.

The first baseball stadium was built in Pittsburgh in 1909, and in Hershey, Pennsylvania, the Chocolate Capital of the world is located in Hershey, Pa. In 1876, the Declaration of Independence was signed in Philadelphia.

Although the Declaration of Independence was signed in Philadelphia, Pennsylvania still produced 75% of the world's oil. For this reason, it is not surprising that the state is full of history! If you want to learn more about the state of Pennsylvania, check out these fun facts for kids.

Apples are grown throughout Pennsylvania. It is the state's official fruit, but there is no official state vegetable. The state is home to the Chocolate Capital of the US, and Hershey is the site of the first Apple World Cup.

Additionally, Hershey is the home of Hershey's chocolate, and is also home to the largest apple plant in the United States. And of course, it is home to the Declaration of Independence, the first piano in the Americas, and the Constitution were all signed in Philadelphia.

Another interesting fact about Pennsylvania is that it is the birthplace of the American revolution. The state is a rich source of history. In 1909, the first baseball stadium was built in Pittsburgh.

In 1776, the first piano was made in Pennsylvania. In the 17th century, the Declaration of Independence was signed in Philadelphia. If you're looking for fun facts about Pennsylvania, read on!

The state has a rich history. In addition to the chocolate industry, Pennsylvania is the Chocolate Capital of the US. It was the first state to build a baseball stadium in 1776. In fact, it has become the Chocolate Capital of the US.

Its history also includes the Declaration of Independence and the first computer in the world. This state was the birthplace of the computer. In fact, there's no shortage of facts about the state.

The state is rich in history. Its capital, Philadelphia, was the first state in the United States to be named. The first baseball stadium in the country was in Pittsburgh. The first computer was created in Pennsylvania in 1946.

In addition to the first piano, the state's Declaration of Independence was signed in Philadelphia. The Declaration of Independence was also written in Pennsylvania. So, if you have kids, you might want to start exploring the many things the keystone state has to offer.

The state has several symbols. Children can identify Pennsylvania cities, states, and counties by looking for these symbols on a map. They can also learn about the climate of the state, which is one of the reasons it is the Chocolate Capital of the US.

Its rivers are abundant and have a rich history. Besides, the state of Philadelphia is the Chocolate Capital of the US. Moreover, the first computer was invented in Philadelphia in 1646. In addition to these, Pennsylvania also became the home of the first piano in the United States.

The deer is the state animal of Pennsylvania. They have been living in the state for thousands of years. They play a vital role in field and forest horticulture in the state. The deer also play an important role in regulating the plant population and food webs.

The Pennsylvania State Motto was adopted in 1776. The State Song was adopted in 1937. The firefly is the state insect. If you visit the area, be sure to learn about the different symbols.

Lightning Source UK Ltd.
Milton Keynes UK
UKHW050809010323
417806UK00010B/148